GHOSTS

BY
JOHN GUY

WHAT IS A GHOST?

Nobody really knows what a ghost is. Despite the long history of recorded sightings, no basic facts have ever been agreed. Modern researchers continue to investigate the subject, but until more is known, the question of whether or not ghosts exist remains largely a matter of faith. Perhaps the most persistent belief is that ghosts are spirits of the dead. This inevitably links the subject with the larger issues of religious belief, cultural superstitions and scientific theory. Whatever our views, the numerous accounts of extraordinary ghostly sightings and events makes this fascinating phenomenen hard to ignore. Why are there reports of ghosts right across the globe, and what truth lies behind these strange sightings?

TRICKS & PRANKS

Many photographs of ghosts have proven to be fakes. Ghostly pictures were popular at the end of the nineteenth century when photography was a new technology. The easiest photographic trick is that of double exposure. This is when two separate shots are taken on the same piece of film, resulting in one image being superimposed over another.

PERCEPTIONS

The image of a ghost that comes to mind for most people is a pathetic figure, clothed in a white gown, rattling chains and perhaps dragging a ball and manacle behind it. In reality, such an obvious manifestation is rare. Most ghosts seem to appear only once, usually at the moment of their death, and never return to haunt their former home. Many people who claim to have seen a ghost report the experience as a positive and uplifting one. They only feel fear as the ghost begins to materialize.

THE AFTERLIFE

Throughout history, most cultures have believed in some form of afterlife. The ancient Egyptians made elaborate preparations for the journey into the afterlife by mummifying and preserving a body after death. The Christian Church promises resurrection of the human soul after death. Ghosts are sometimes thought to be souls or spirits trapped on Earth, unable to pass over to the spiritual plane.

ALTERED STATES OF AWARENESS

Drugs, such as alcohol, marijuana (right), LSD and cocaine can have a profound effect on the brain and sometimes cause hallucinations. However, it is sometimes claimed that the drugs, by altering the user's state of awareness, allow the human brain to see presences which are always there but are not normally visible to us. Ghosts have sometimes been accounted for in this way.

FANTASTIC LIGHTS

Some ghosts may be attributable to natural phenomena. In the past, fantastic lights such as the *aurora borealis* around the North Pole could have been mistaken for spiritual visitations. A common phenomenon known as will-o'-the-wisp has often been mistaken for ghosts. For centuries, these mysterious pale lights have been seen hovering over marshland. Rather than spirits of the dead, they are the spontaneous combustion of marsh gasses.

FOOD FOR THOUGHT

People on the brink of death have experienced seeing a tunnel of ephemeral white light apparently beckoning them into the afterlife. Recent scientific research suggests a physical rather than a spiritual explanation for these near-death experiences. Sensory deprivation is known to produce hallucinations in the brain. Also, lack of oxygen to the brain could stimulate cells in the cortex which would induce the tunnel and white light effect.

ASTRAL PROJECTION

Most religions believe in a spirit world (or astral plane) to which the souls of the dead return. It is not a separate place in the heavens but is thought to exist all around us at a level of consciousness of which we are normally unaware. The astral body, or spirit of a person, is said to leave the body during sleep and at death to enter this other level of existence. Ghosts may be astral projections of dead people that have become trapped between this world and the next. Until released in some way, they are unable to pass fully into the spirit world.

FOOD FOR THOUGHT

Maybe victims of violent crimes, such as murder, generate an excess of chemicals such as adrenaline or a high charge of electrical activity within their bodies. In some way this may impart an image or energy field into the surrounding air. Under the right conditions, this image might be seen like a hologram, but it is merely an image with no physical substance.

ISLE OF THE BLESSED

In Celtic mythology, when King Arthur was about to die he was transported in a boat to Avalon, Isle of the Blessed. According to legend, Arthur did not die but recovered and would return to fight the enemies of his country whenever he was needed. Unable to rest lest he be called upon, the ghost of Arthur has sometimes been seen at the Cam valley in Somerset, the supposed site of the king's last Earthly battle.

RESTLESS SOULS

The most common reason given for a ghost manifesting itself is that the spirit or soul of the dead person is troubled and unable to rest. This state of transience is believed to have many causes, but all are in some way connected to a sense of injustice, or perhaps guilt that in life the person did not do all they could have to protect someone. Injustice might be felt by the victim of a violent murder who returns again and again to the scene of the crime, apparently unable to rest until the murderer has been revealed. Alternatively, a ghost might simply be someone who was not ready to die and felt aggrieved that their time on Earth had been cut short.

PHANTOM CARGO

In Papua New Guinea, natives are often seen scanning the horizon for 'phantom cargo'. They wait for dead relatives to come in great canoes (nowadays, ships and planes too) full of goods that will enrich their lives. In the past, missionaries who brought with them artefacts from the civilized world were sometimes allowed to settle in Papua because the natives mistook them for the ghosts of their dead ancestors.

HEADLESS HAUNTINGS

Headless ghosts are common, presumably because the person felt a strong sense of injustice about meeting such a violent end. In the past, the Tower of London was the scene of many executions and is reputed to be the single most haunted building in the world. Similarly, in Paris at the time of the French Revolution (1789-1799), the site of the executions is reputedly haunted by several headless ghosts, including Louis XVI and Marie Antoinette.

MYTHICAL GODS

In Nordic mythology, one of the most feared apparitions was Odin, the god of war. Leading a pack of dogs on the 'Wild Hunt', Odin rides across the night sky in search of lost souls. The apparition usually foretold an impending death.

UNKNOWN FORCES

Most ghosts appear to be benign and cause no physical harm. However, some spirits seem to be far from passive and can inflict actual bodily injuries or, in extreme cases, death. The most common form of such malevolent behaviour is poltergeist activity. There are also many reports of people falling victim to invisible assailants. One extreme case in 1761 in Ventimiglia, Italy, involved a woman who was attacked by an unseen force. Her body was quite literally torn apart in the presence of her four companions who remained unharmed.

HAIR TODAY, GONE TOMORROW

Between 1876-9 the province of Nanking, in China, suffered a strange yet oddly recurring phenomenon in Chinese history. An invisible assailant ran amok cutting off people's pigtails. Sometimes a shadowy figure was seen, briefly, while at other times the hair was invisibly grabbed from behind and shorn off. Similar happenings were reported in Canada in 1899 and in London in 1922.

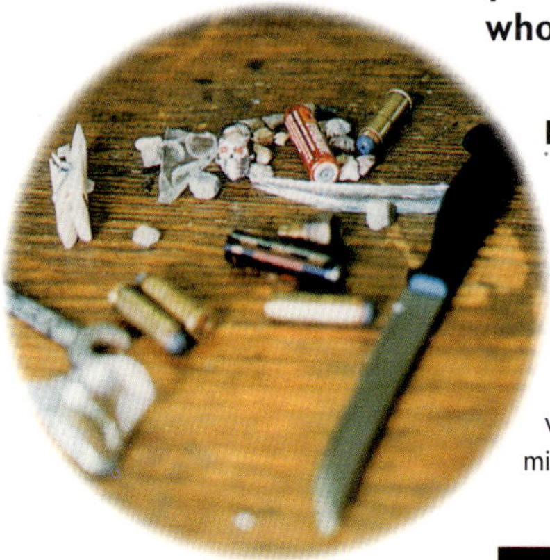

POLTERGEISTS

Poltergeist activity often includes objects being hurled through the air, but sometimes they also appear apparently out of nowhere. In 1998, all the items shown here 'fell' into a house in the Northern Territory of Australia within a period of 2-3 hours. The knife flew past an investigator who was in the house at the time, narrowly missing his ear.

FOOD FOR THOUGHT

There is plenty of evidence of malevolent poltergeist activity but the source of this 'power' remains a mystery. Much poltergeist activity is centred around young teenage girls at the time when their bodies are undergoing immense physical changes. The girls may themselves be the source of the poltergeist activity, as a result of heightened mental and chemical activity affecting the environment around them.

CAUGHT ON CAMERA

This still from 1967 video footage taken in Rosenheim, Germany, shows a light fixture in a solicitor's office swinging unaided. No physical cause could be attributed to the phenomenon. The telephone system also behaved strangely. All four of the office telephones would suddenly ring without reason, and strange power surges were recorded. Sigmund Adam, the solicitor, called in experts to help. The source of these mysterious happenings seemed to be his clerk, a 19-year-old woman. When she left, the activity stopped.

HOUSE CLEARANCE

The furniture in this house in Dodlestone, Chester, was repeatedly piled into one corner of the room by an unknown force while the owners were out of the room. On one occasion in 1983, computer messages were also received, purportedly transmitted by a man living in the sixteenth century. Perhaps this is a case of parallel worlds where people from other timespans or dimensions appear to be sharing the same space as ourselves.

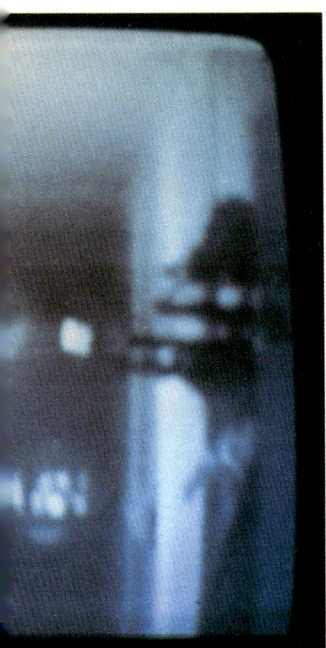

BODILY HARM

In 1926, this 13-year-old Romanian girl Eleonore Zugun suffered horrific injuries at the hands of an invisible force. Witnesses describe seeing her throat being squeezed as though she were being throttled. On other occasions, bite and scratch marks appeared spontaneously on her face and neck.

HEAVENLY VISIONS

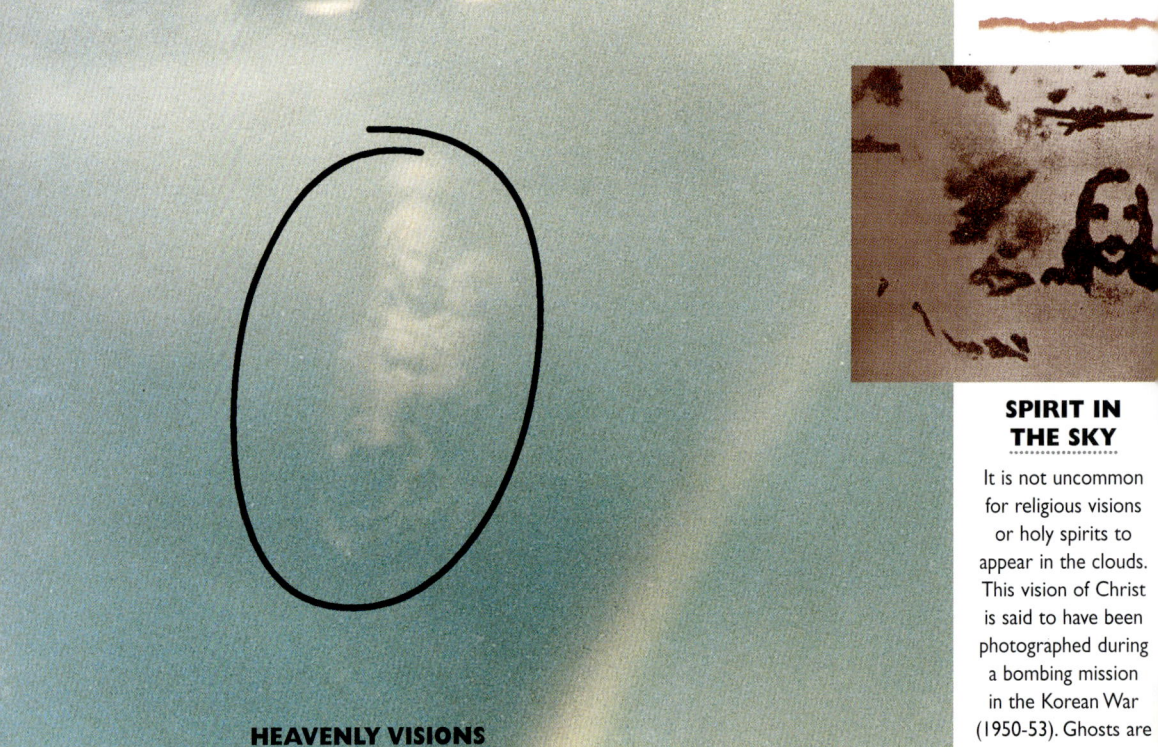

From time to time, someone reports seeing a miraculous vision. These visions come in a variety of forms including dreams, ghostly appearances, and miraculous images. In 1980, Mrs Ivy Wilson photographed this rainbow at Woombye in south-eastern Queensland, Australia. When she had the film developed she noticed this image of the Virgin Mary and child. The photograph was not taken through glass, so it could not have been a reflection.

SPIRIT IN THE SKY

It is not uncommon for religious visions or holy spirits to appear in the clouds. This vision of Christ is said to have been photographed during a bombing mission in the Korean War (1950-53). Ghosts are often described as if they are made of the same matter as clouds, and like clouds they can appear for a few moments before vaporizing into thin air. The soul has also been likened to a cloud that vaporizes as it leaves the body.

HOLY GHOSTS

The Church is usually associated with banishing unwelcome spirits but it also has a fair share of its own ghosts. Many of these apparitions take the form of miraculous images, or visions of Christ, the Virgin Mary or the saints. Apart from these religious visions, the Church tends to explain ghosts as restless spirits whose souls, for one reason or another, are unable to pass over into the afterlife; and they blame the unruly behaviour of poltergeists on the Devil. Most religions classify good and bad spirits in much the same way. The Christian Church calls the spirit of God the Holy Ghost.

METHODIST IN THEIR MADNESS

Towards the end of the seventeenth century, the Wesley family, founders of the Methodist Church, moved into the Old Rectory at Epworth in Yorkshire, England. The rectory became the centre of much activity and religious fervour. This may have unsettled a Catholic spirit because, for a short period during 1715-16, the house suffered what may have been poltergeist activity. Incidents were many and varied, including a corn grinder and mechanical spit that started up unaided, the sounds of a rocking cradle, mysterious knocking noises and doors that suddenly flew open. Headless animals were seen, and members of the family were hurled against walls. The activity gradually subsided but incidents there still occasionally occur.

GETTING THE HABIT

Everywhere in the world, there are ruined churches or abbeys allegedly haunted by monks and nuns. A Siberian peasant monk, Grigori Rasputin is said to haunt the old royal palace in Moscow. Having gained the confidence of Nicholas II and Alexandra, Rasputin virtually ruled Russia prior to the Revolution. He made many enemies and was murdered by a group of noblemen in 1916. His ghost still walks the corridors of power, supposedly seeking revenge.

DREAMTIME

Aboriginal Australians treat their dead relatives with extreme reverence. They have no fear of death, and the ghosts of their dead are welcome to join in their rituals and celebrations. Aboriginals periodically perform magic rituals to renew their relationship with their dead ancestors who are encouraged to revisit their earthly tribal lands.

FOOD FOR THOUGHT

Seeing visions in cloud shapes has a rational explanation. Known as eidetic images, such visions can be exceptionally vivid but are thought to be recalled from something previously seen. If we stare long and hard at some unrelated surface, many of us will begin to see things such as faces among the patterns on wallpaper or in the flickering flames of a fire, or images in the sky. The human mind works hard to 'read' what is being seen and may eventually interpret abstract shapes as a familiar object or perhaps a desired supernatural being.

FOOD FOR THOUGHT

Associating ghosts with the Devil and haunting music were probably ploys used by early Church authorities as they attempted to woo people away from pagan religions to follow the new true faith (as they saw it) of Christianity. Many European legends tell of ghosts haunting the ancient standing stone monuments which were centres of pagan religions. Some say the stones themselves are the petrified remains of dancers who were turned to stone by the Devil as they danced on the Sabbath.

THINGS THAT GO BUMP IN THE NIGHT

Ghosts are often accompanied by strange sounds. Indeed, some ghosts seem only to be audible spirits who never manifest themselves in any visible form. Sounds associated with the earthly life of the ghost are common; so too is music. Sometimes, especially with poltergeists, a haunting is accompanied by obscene or blasphemous language. This is often voiced through living people, as if the ghost were using them as a vehicle to express its anger. Audible ghosts are often accompanied by a sense of foreboding as if they are predicting some tragic event. In Irish folklore, wailing banshees are female spirits said to warn of an impending death. Such spirits are common in many other cultures, including India and South America.

A PLANE MYSTERY

The American musician Glen Miller is generally held to be the finest band leader of his day. On 15th December 1944, he took a plane from England to Paris to arrange a series of concerts for the US troops in France. The plane disappeared into thick fog and was never seen again. Several reports have described the outline of a small aircraft flying in the area where the plane is believed to have gone down. The sightings are accompanied by the ghostly sounds of a trombone.

THE DEVIL'S MUSIC

In more religious times, ghosts were often seen as the Earthly manifestation of the Devil himself. They were considered to be evil, especially if music accompanied the manifestation. There are many old stories of the Devil attending festivities and disguising himself as a musician to tempt revellers to dance on the Sabbath (seventh day of the week, a holy day). He played demonic music until the dancers either dropped from exhaustion or died.

PLAINTIFF SONG

Mermaids are creatures said to have no soul. In some stories, ghosts are transformed into mermaids and condemned to roam the Earth in search of a soul. Legend tells of the sad, haunting songs these creatures use to lure people to them. Scientists have recently advanced a theory that these 'ghosts of the sea' are no more than mirages formed by the air distortions caused by differing sea temperatures.

THE DRUMMER OF TEDWORTH

At Tedworth in Wiltshire, England, a famous ghost has been making regular appearances since the seventeenth century. The ghostly outline of a figure in the full military uniform of the day has often been seen on the old road to Devizes, and heard playing a drum.

SCENTED SPIRITS

Some ghosts make their presence felt by scents and odours, as well as by sound. At Cotehele House in Cornwall, England, several ghosts have been reported over the years, including that of a white lady. Ghostly music is sometimes heard but visitors often ask what the strong herbal fragrance is that seems to permeate the whole house. The scent seems to come and go at random at all times of the day.

CITY OF GOD

Whilst camped outside Rome in AD 312, Emperor Constantine saw a vision of a fiery cross in the midday sky. An inscription on it urged him to attack the city. He carried out the attack and was victorious. In gratitude to the holy spirit which he claimed to have seen, he ordered that Christianity become the official religion of the Roman Empire.

CUSTER'S LAST STAND

In June 1876, American Civil War hero General Custer was killed fighting the Sioux Indians at the Battle of Little Bighorn. One month earlier, as Custer had ridden out of Fort Abraham Lincoln at the start of the expedition, people in the fort saw half the regiment apparently rise up into the sky and then vanish. It may have been a mirage caused by the heat of the sun, but about half the 7th Cavalry were subsequently massacred in the battle.

SPECTRAL ARMIES

In the past, when belief in myth and legend was greater than it is today, ghosts tended to be of a more spectacular nature. Visions of gods or heroic figures would appear, and spectral armies fighting battles in the sky were once quite a common occurrence. Today, such visions are rare; in modern hauntings, people tend to see just one ghost. This would seem to indicate a link between the kind of apparition seen and the background and experience of the person who sees it. There are stories of King Arthur and the ancient gods Odin and Thor fighting great ghostly battles. These spectral events could have been mirages of actual battles, while others were perhaps portents of battles yet to be fought.

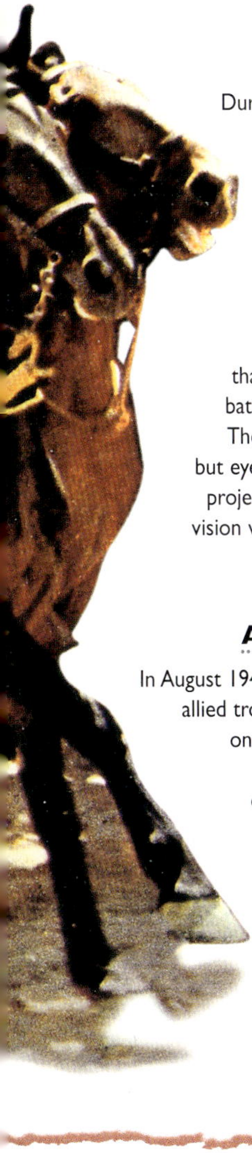

DRAKE'S DRUM

Sir Francis Drake (1540-96) used a drum to muster the crew of the *Golden Hind* for battle. According to legend, Drake promised on his deathbed to return and fight for England if ever the drum were beaten at the approach of an enemy. During World War II, stories circulated of warships being miraculously saved from disaster after the ghostly sounds of drumming were heard. However, Drake's drum has never been carried aboard any ship since its return to England in the sixteenth century.

BOWMEN OF MONS

During World War I (1914-1918), the first battle fought by British forces was at Mons in Belgium, where they were grossly outnumbered by the German Army. A report in the newspapers told of a miraculous vision that appeared in the sky above the battlefield, urging on the British troops.

The report claimed the vision was St George and his bowmen, but eyewitnesses from both sides told of an army carrying swords, projected onto the sky like a film. No sounds were heard but the vision was witnessed by many individuals on the battlefield, and has been interpreted by some as divine intervention.

ACTION REPLAY

In August 1942, during World War II, allied troops launched an attack on the German-held town of Dieppe on the coast of Normandy in France. It was a prelude to the D-Day landings and the mission was a success. Nine years later, two women on holiday near Dieppe were woken early one morning by the sound of gunfire. For the next three hours, they listened in stunned silence as the battle of nine years before was re-enacted. Their accounts were afterwards compared to official records of the battle and found to be very similar.

FOOD FOR THOUGHT

The intensity of a life-or-death battle inevitably causes the release of large amounts of adrenaline in the participants. Stories such as the Bowmen of Mons may have been the result of mass hysteria, or born out of a collective memory of some long-past scene. People often see what they want to see. Three different observers of the same event, say a soldier, a priest, and a scientist will each explain it in terms they relate to. The soldier may see an army of ghost soldiers in the sky; the priest the divine light of God; while the scientist may see ball lightning or interpret the others' visions as products of overwrought minds.

FOOD FOR THOUGHT

The most obvious explanation for ghosts seen at sea is that sailors, subjected to long voyages often in rough waters, can become disoriented or unbalanced. This could distort the sensory perception of seamen and lead them to believe they are actually seeing things that are not there, in much the same way as an hallucination.

THE FLYING DUTCHMAN

In 1680, the *Flying Dutchman* set sail from Amsterdam for Batavia in the Dutch East Indies. The ship was severely damaged in a violent storm off the Cape of Good Hope but the captain refused to turn back. His arrogance and blasphemous behaviour was said to have caused God to condemn him to sail the seas forever. Now considered an ill omen, the phantom ship has since been seen many times, including by the future king of England, George V, in 1881.

PHANTOM SHIPS

Over the centuries, the world's oceans have been the scene of many shipping disasters, and the loss of life has often given rise to tales of ghosts and phantom ships. One area particularly associated with mystery is the **Bermuda Triangle** in the north Atlantic. Hundreds of ships (and planes) have simply disappeared there without trace and several ghost ships have been reported in the area. When sightings of phantom ships are reported by credible witnesses such as King George V, who as a young naval officer sighted the *Flying Dutchman*, we are forced to take the stories seriously rather than dismiss them as a delusion of sailors who have drunk too much rum.

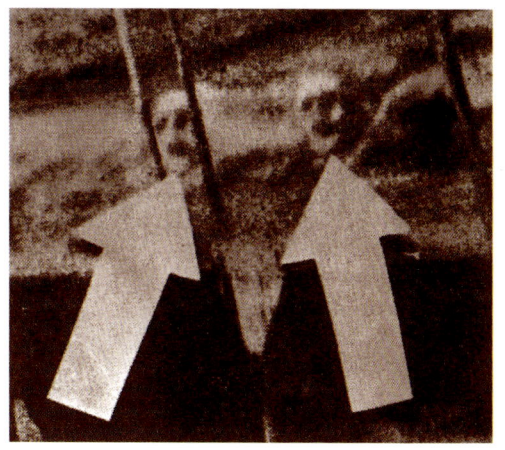

ALL AT SEA

This rare photograph is purported to show the images of two dead seamen as witnessed by the ship's entire crew. In the 1920s, the oil tanker SS *Watertown* was sailing from the Pacific coast of America to the Panama Canal. Two of the crew died in an accident and were buried at sea. The next day and for several days after, two phantom faces which resembled the dead crewmen were seen in the waves behind the ship. They always appeared in the same position for a few moments, then disappeared. The likenesses appeared during the next two voyages of the ship but were never seen again.

AIR SHIPS

From all corners of the globe there have been reports of mysterious airships; not the great gas-filled zeppelins of the early twentieth century, but wooden galleons in full sail drifting across the sky. One such apparition was witnessed in Papua New Guinea in 1959 by the entire staff of a religious mission.

SEA RESCUE

In 1895, Joshua Slocum, the first man to sail round the world single-handed, claimed to have been rescued by a sixteenth-century ghost. Taken ill during a ferocious storm in the Azores, the American seaman collapsed on his bunk. When he woke, Slocum saw at the helm of his ship, the *Spray*, a seaman who said he was the pilot of the *Pinta*, a caravel (like this replica) that had sailed with Columbus in 1492. The apparition could be dismissed as delirium, except that the *Spray* had remained precisely on course for some 90 miles (144 km).

A VENGEFUL GHOST?

In 1908, the British warship HMS *Gladiator* (left) sank in Portsmouth harbour after colliding with the American steam liner, *St Paul*, with the loss of 27 lives. Incredibly, exactly ten years later to the hour, the *St Paul* inexplicably capsized in the Hudson River in New York and sank with the loss of four lives. Claims of sabotage were rife but because of the amazing coincidence of date and time, many believed that the ghost of a dead seaman from the *Gladiator* was responsible.

LITERARY SPOOKING

People who have never seen a ghost find it very hard to believe in them, but many of us keep an open mind about their existence. However, we positively enjoy the inclusion of fictional ghosts in books and plays. A ghostly haunting can be a useful device used by authors to force a character to atone for some misdemeanour. In such plots, the haunted characters usually become so eaten-up by their sense of guilt that they cause their own downfall. These literary ghosts can take on a real and familiar presence in our imagination almost to the point of our believing in them. This may help to keep alive the possibility of ghosts really existing.

GHOST STORIES

Sometimes ghosts were used as a literary device to put across an idea or message, especially in politically sensitive times when the depiction of contemporary events might have been prohibited by a repressive regime. This Japanese woodcut is a piece of veiled war propaganda expressed by having a ghost appear to the Samurai warrior Kingo Chunagon Hideaki during the nineteenth-century civil wars in Japan.

GHOULISH GHOSTS

Ghosts are big business. Many films featuring them have drawn huge audiences. Some, like *Casper the Friendly Ghost* (right) and *Ghostbusters,* are light-hearted spoofs, but others, such as *The Exorcist*, are said to be based on real events. *The Exorcist* tells the story of a young girl possessed by the Devil. When the film was shown in a cinema in Australia, several of the audience left before the film had even started because of strange occurrences in the cinema.

GHOSTLY INTERVENTION

Dante's celebrated poem, 'The Divine Comedy' may never have been published were it not for the intervention of his own ghost. When he died in 1321, everyone supposed his epic poem was unfinished because, despite an exhaustive search, the missing part of the manuscript could not be found. One night, however, Dante's ghost appeared to his son, Jacopo, in a dream to reveal the secret hiding place. It has been suggested that Jacopo may have finished the poem himself and used the ploy of the ghost to pass off the work as his father's.

GUILTY CONSCIENCE

Many authors have used a ghost in their plots to make their characters face up to the consequences of past actions. In *A Christmas Carol* by Charles Dickens, Scrooge is visited by the ghosts of Christmases past, present and future to make him atone for being a grasping old miser. Shakespeare used a ghost scene to make Macbeth repent his murder of Banquo. Dickens himself was buried at Westminster Abbey in London, yet his ghost is said to haunt a graveyard in Rochester where the author had wanted to be buried.

FOOD FOR THOUGHT

Humankind seems to thrive on mystery. In the past, religions fulfilled our need to explain what we don't understand. People went in fear of God and believed fervently in demons, evil spirits and the afterlife. Science has explained away many of the mysteries of life and death, leaving some people feeling a spiritual lack without something outside themselves in which to believe. Perhaps being willing to believe in the supernatural is an attempt to fill this void. Also, it is comforting to think there could be some continuance of life after death. Literature and films about ghosts both entertain us and feed an apparent spiritual need, but as far as we know have no basis in fact.

GHOSTLY VISIT

The Swiss psychologist Carl Jung (1875-1961) had a great interest in the afterlife and wrote effusively about it in his autobiography. He claimed, among other things, that the ghost of a recently departed friend had visited him in a dream and taken him on a tour of the friend's study. The following day, Jung visited the man's widow and asked to see the study, which he had never seen. To his amazement, it was exactly as he had envisaged in his dream.

GHOSTLY BEASTS

Animals feature quite prominently in accounts of ghost sightings. Sometimes, ghosts of dead pets appear in much the same way as conventional ghosts. Some ghost animals are seen as harbingers of ill-fortune. Perhaps of more interest is the apparent ability of animals to sense the presence of ghosts before humans are aware of them. This may indicate that animals have a kind of extrasensory perception. Dogs often will not enter a haunted room or, if they do, their hackles will rise as if they detect an intruder. Because animals often possess senses way beyond the normal human range, they may detect the changes to electro-magnetic fields that are often associated with reports of ghosts.

WHITE BIRDS

Although associated with love, peace, and with life itself, white doves are sometimes the harbingers of impending death. Ghostly white birds have been seen fluttering above the beds of those near to death. Sometimes they are seen by the dying person, at other times by independent witnesses, but always they foretell a death in the household. Similar sightings have been reported from widely different places such as Ireland and Japan.

FOOD FOR THOUGHT

When confronted by something unexpected, most people react with fear. Large black cats have been seen in locations around the world where such wild animals should not exist. It is all too easy to assume such beasts are in some way supernatural. However, a growing body of evidence suggests that large feral cats, such as black panthers, may have escaped from zoos or private collections and somehow managed to survive in urban areas.

THE DEVIL

Most cultures of the world have their equivalent of the Devil as known in Christianity. He usually represents the antithesis of all that is good. To see him is to bring bad luck or death. He often takes the form of a creature who is half man, half beast. Many people believe that all animal ghosts are really the Devil in disguise.

PHANTOM CANINES

The most commonly seen animal phantoms are black dogs which are usually, but not always, associated with evil. They are often believed to be affiliated with the Devil and those who encounter them are frequently injured. Black dog manifestations are also said to predict an impending death. However, it used to be the custom in medieval Europe to bury a dog in new graveyards to protect the souls of the dead.

SACRED RATS

The temple of Karai Ma at Bikaner in the Indian state of Rajasthan is infested with rats. Karai Ma is the goddess of a caste of professional poets, called Charans. Whenever a Charan dies he is believed to return to the temple as a rat, and when a rat dies it is said to return as a poet.

GHOSTLY FELINE

Not all ghostly sightings of animals are of a sinister nature. At a house called King John's Hunting Lodge in Somerset, England, the ghost of a friendly tabby cat (probably the much-loved pet of a previous owner) has often been seen. It appears to enter a first-floor panelled room through a closed door and happily curls up on the floor before disappearing.

SCREECHING OWLS

Owls have traditionally been associated with death. Ghosts of owls that appear at the window of a house and then mysteriously disappear are thought to foretell a death in the family.

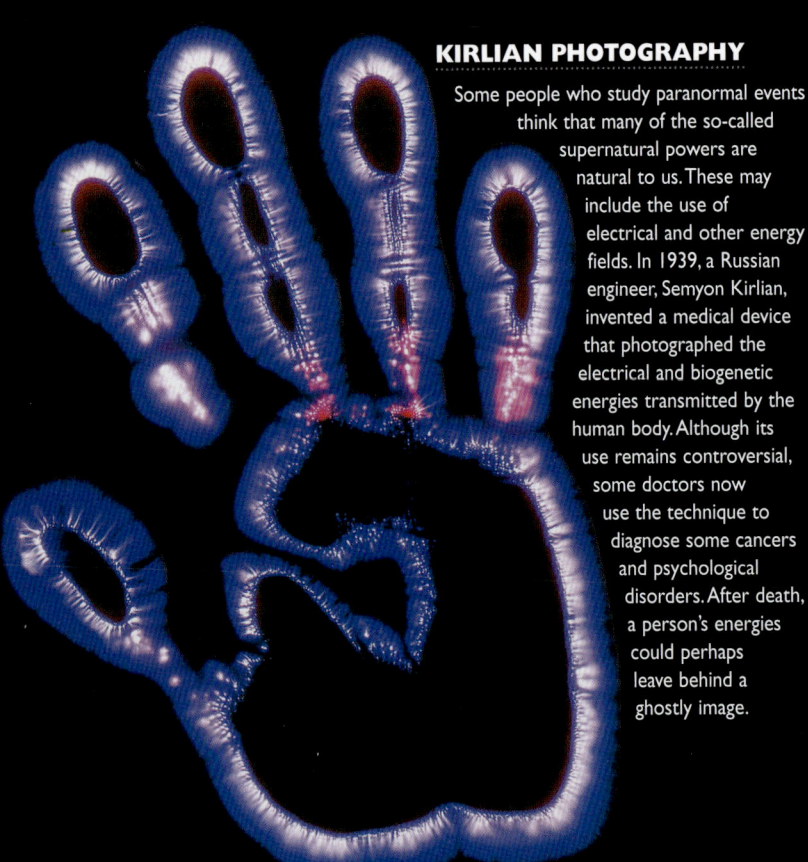

KIRLIAN PHOTOGRAPHY

Some people who study paranormal events think that many of the so-called supernatural powers are natural to us. These may include the use of electrical and other energy fields. In 1939, a Russian engineer, Semyon Kirlian, invented a medical device that photographed the electrical and biogenetic energies transmitted by the human body. Although its use remains controversial, some doctors now use the technique to diagnose some cancers and psychological disorders. After death, a person's energies could perhaps leave behind a ghostly image.

A SHADOW OF OURSELVES

Another popular theory is that ghosts are human aura somehow trapped on this Earthly plane long after the people have died. Apparent each of us radiates an invisib electro-magnetic energy fie which in the past only peop such as clairvoyants were ab to detect. Modern science h confirmed that the human be emanates a field of energy t could be what has been described as an aura.

THE LITTLE PEOPLE

Folklore is full of tales of mythical creatures such as fairies, elves, and dwarves. Although these 'little people' are seen as purely fictional nowadays, it is possible that their origins could be traced to distant memories of creatures who did actually exist alongside man. Perhaps they still do and remain mostly elusive, but when they are seen we interpret their presence as ghostly.

BEINGS FROM OTHER WORLDS

There are many similarities between the reported sightings of ghosts and those of aliens coming to Earth in unidentified flying objects (UFOs). Both are elusive, visible only at certain times and by particular people. Perhaps they are different aspects of the same phenomenon. 'Aliens' may be manifestations of human spirits from Earth rather than from outer space.

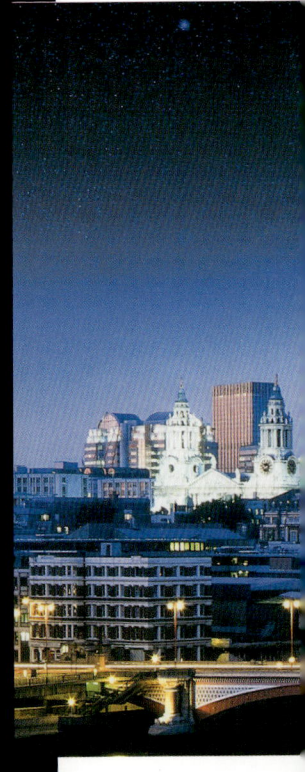

PARALLEL WORLDS

Ghosts may not be the spirits of dead people from this world but are perhaps beings from a parallel world. They are not normally visible to our human senses but occasionally, when conditions are right, we may catch a glimpse of them. The idea of other worlds existing undetected alongside our own is a very old one. Some people like to think the creatures of folklore and mythology are not simply the product of human imagination but recalled memories of a time past when there was contact between our worlds. Parallels can be drawn to the animal kingdom in which creatures with a different range of senses to our own see an entirely different world to us, even though we occupy the same space and time on Earth.

CIRCLE OF HANDS

A long-established method of getting in touch with the spirit world is to conduct a seance. A group of people sit round a table in a quiet, darkened room. A medium, someone who is sensitive to the spirit world, acts as a go-between. Rituals are performed until the medium makes contact with a spirit and receives a message on behalf of one of the participants.

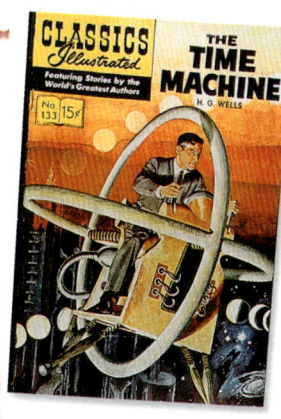

TIME TRAVEL

For centuries mankind has been fascinated by the idea of the past, present and future co-existing in parallel worlds, normally invisible to one another. Authors, such as H.G. Wells (1866-1946), and filmmakers have often used the idea. Although a controversial issue, the physicist Albert Einstein (1879-1955) used his theory of relativity to prove that the existence of parallel time and space is possible. If it is, then sightings of ghosts may be glimpses of people's past or future lives in another dimension.

FOOD FOR THOUGHT

Various forms of telepathy may be possible between some people, especially if they are closely related. They may be able to communicate thoughts without actually speaking. Perhaps mediums can pick up thoughts and feelings about a dead friend or relative from participants at a seance. If so, they would of course be accurate. However, mediums may just be excellent judges of character who, over the years, have become expert at telling people what they want to hear.

THIS HAUNTED ISLE

For some reason, the British Isles appear to be the focus of a great deal of supernatural activity. Their populations have recorded more sightings of UFOs, ghosts and other strange phenomena than any other region of comparable size in the world. Every year, there are almost more sightings of ghosts reported in Britain than in the rest of the world put together, making Britain the unofficial ghost capital of the world. Whatever the reasons for this high level of apparent spectral activity, it does mean that there is a wealth of material from all periods in history to investigate.

MULTIPLE HAUNTINGS

Many sites in Britain are haunted by more than one ghost. Destroyed by fire in 1939, Borley Rectory in Essex was haunted by several ghosts including a poltergeist, although doubt has now been cast upon their authenticity. Pluckley is said to be the most haunted village in Kent or perhaps in all England. The most frequently seen ghost is the Red Lady, who haunts the local churchyard shown above, but there are at least a dozen others.

FEAR OF THE UNKNOWN

Ancient sites, such as the standing stones of Stonehenge in England, are often said to be haunted by spirits that protect their sanctity. One of the most common of these is the Devil himself. It is said that anyone who desecrates the monument will meet an untimely end — perhaps being turned to stone.

THE WHITE LADY

Almost every castle in Britain is said to be haunted, many by unknown spirits. Rochester Castle in Kent is haunted by the ghost of Lady Blanche de Warenne. During a siege of the castle in 1264, she was accosted on the battlements by a rejected suitor, Gilbert de Clare. Ralph de Capo, to whom she was engaged, shot an arrow at her assailant. Deflected by de Clare's armour it unfortunately killed Lady Blanche. Her ghost is now said to walk the battlements every year on the anniversary of her death.

LORE AND ORDER

At Bramshill House in Hampshire, now used as a police training college, there have been so many ghostly encounters that even the worldly-wise police officers have accepted that the house must be haunted. In addition to the more usual ghosts, there are apparently rooms in the house that dogs will not enter and even a path in the grounds that is haunted. One of the more pathetic of the several apparitions that haunt the house is a young girl who accidentally suffocated in a chest during a game of hide-and-seek one Christmas.

FOOD FOR THOUGHT

Well-known for their fertile imaginations, the British have produced some of the world's greatest works of literature and scientific invention. Perhaps their lively minds are all too willing to see mystery where none exists, embellish it, and pass it on as myth. The often murky weather conditions of the British Isles could account for some of the strange shadowy shapes that are sometimes thought to be ghosts.

GLOBAL HAUNTINGS

Although certain places seem to be a focus for supernatural activity, nowhere on Earth is off-limits to ghosts. Wherever there are people, you will find accounts of ghosts. It seems that many ghosts repeatedly act out an action replay of a particular event in their previous life, oblivious to all observers. Others are apparently benevolent and sometimes try to warn strangers of impending danger. However, occasionally ghosts can be malevolent.

SEEING DOUBLE

There are numerous stories of people who apparently have a double and are seen in two places at once. In 1845, in Livaria, Russia, one woman's double image actually appeared alongside her. A school teacher called Madame Sages was able to project an image of herself beyond her body. She used the technique in her classroom to maintain discipline, and while her ghostly image sat in front of the class she would walk around or write on the blackboard. Her actions were witnessed not only by her pupils, but also by her colleagues who eventually asked for her dismissal.

THE SWEET SMELL OF VIOLETS

During the Zulu wars in South Africa last century, the Prince Imperial of France was killed. His body was returned to his family for burial and a cairn of stones erected as a memorial on the site where he had died.

The following year, the prince's mother, Eugenie, wished to visit the battlefield where her son had died, but she could not find the memorial. Whilst searching the undergrowth she became aware of the scent of violets, which had been his favourite flower, and was guided to the cairn.

CAR 42, WHERE ARE YOU?

The first Grand Prix to be held in Japan after World War II was in 1963 at the Suzuka circuit in Nagoya. The favourite was Masao Asano driving a car emblazoned with the number 42. During the race, Asano's car went out of control and he suffered a fatal crash. In Japanese the number 42 translates as *shi ni*, which means 'to die'. Racing officials afterwards banned the use of the number 42 but in the following year's Grand Prix event, marshals checking the cars as they passed noticed that a car bearing the number 42 was seen in 8 out of the 25 laps.

CAUGHT IN TIME

In August 1901, two women visiting the Palace of Versailles walked towards the small private château of the queen of France, Marie Antoinette (1755-93). Along the way, they sensed an oppressive atmosphere and passed strangely attired gardeners. A woman was sketching in the garden as they arrived.

On a subsequent visit, the layout of the palace and gardens was different and they were convinced they must have slipped back in time on the previous occasion. They later identified the lady sketching as Marie Antoinette. Remarkably, the gardeners an the lady had stared at them, as though they were actually the

COFFINS THAT MOVED

In 1808, in Christ Church, Barbados, the family crypt of a Mrs Goddard was bought by a plantation-owning family, the Chases. They buried two daughters in the stone tomb, but when it was reopened in 1812 to bury Mr Chase who, like one of his daughters, had committed suicide, the heavy lead coffins inside were found upended. The same happened at two more burials. In 1819, the Governor of Barbados ordered the tomb to be sealed as it was creating fear among the local population. Following noises from within the tomb, it was reopened and the coffins were again in disarray, except Mrs Goddard's. There was no sign of forced entry.

FOOD FOR THOUGHT

Human intervention could account for many supposed hauntings. In the case of the coffins that apparently moved by themselves, they could simply have been thrown into disarray by surviving relatives of the previous owner of the crypt, who might have resented the intrusion of strangers into the family grave. Tired minds can also create a dream-like state so that we can easily become confused between the real world and that of daydreams, believing that we have seen things when, in fact, there is nothing there.

A HOUSE BUILT BY GHOSTS

Winchester House in California, was built to appease the spirit world. William Winchester, founder of the famous arms company, died in 1881. His widow, who had recently also lost their only child, became troubled by spirits. A spiritualist told her that the souls of all those killed by a Winchester rifle had banded together to seek revenge. The spirits insisted she build a house to their specifications without rest until she died. In 1884, Mrs Winchester bought a small farmhouse. Day and night for the rest of her life, she expanded it according to the bizarre instructions of the spirits. It has many strange features such as staircases that rise to the ceiling and doors that lead nowhere.

DAY OF THE DEAD

In Mexico, the Purepecha Indians perform elaborate ceremonies not only to venerate the memories of dead ancestors, but also to actively encourage their spirits to appear. In November each year the dead have divine permission to visit their living relatives during the Day of the Dead celebrations.

FOOD FOR THOUGHT

Exorcisms are commonly performed by priests of all religions to rid people and places of evil spirits. This could be a simple matter of auto-suggestion (mind over matter). Superstitious people can be possessed by a spirit only because they are willing to believe such a thing is possible. Just as people can convince themselves they are possessed, they can go to a priest in whom they have absolute faith and likewise convince themselves that the priest is able to exorcise the evil spirit. In reality, they were probably never possessed at all; it was all in their own mind.

GLOBAL ATTITUDES

Cultures around the world have different attitudes to ghosts. Westerners tend to fear ghosts as the restless spirits of the dead, whereas in many supposedly less sophisticated cultures the ghosts of ancestors are celebrated and welcomed. However, if the spirits of the dead are in some way violated they might exact some form of revenge. In 1942, a man named Adrian Brooks was posted as District Officer at Kasama in what is now Zambia. He inadvertently violated the sacred burial ground of the chiefs of a local tribe, the Wemba, by taking photographs of the site. Witch doctors warned him that he had angered the spirits of their leaders and their ghosts would return to kill him. He scoffed at the warning but three days later he suffered a bizarre fatal accident when a flag pole fell on him.

SPIRIT POSSESSION

In Voodoo ceremonies, participants actively encourage the ghosts or spirits of the dead to possess them. The rhythmic drumming sends dancers into such a frenzy that they go into a trance-like state. The combination of powerful auto-suggestion from the witch doctor and hallucinogenic drugs work together to produce a powerful effect.

DEMONIC POSSESSION

Exorcisms are performed in all religions to banish unwelcome spirits. This Dayak shaman from Borneo in Indonesia is performing an exorcism on an unfortunate individual who has been possessed by a demon.

HALLOWE'EN

In ancient times, 31 October marked the end of the old year when the veil between this world and the afterlife was at its thinnest. On this night, the spirits of the dead were able to leave their graves and wander the Earth. The Christian Church adopted the festival as Allhallows Eve and despite its pagan origins the night is still celebrated, especially in America where it involves the light-hearted ritual of 'trick or treat'.

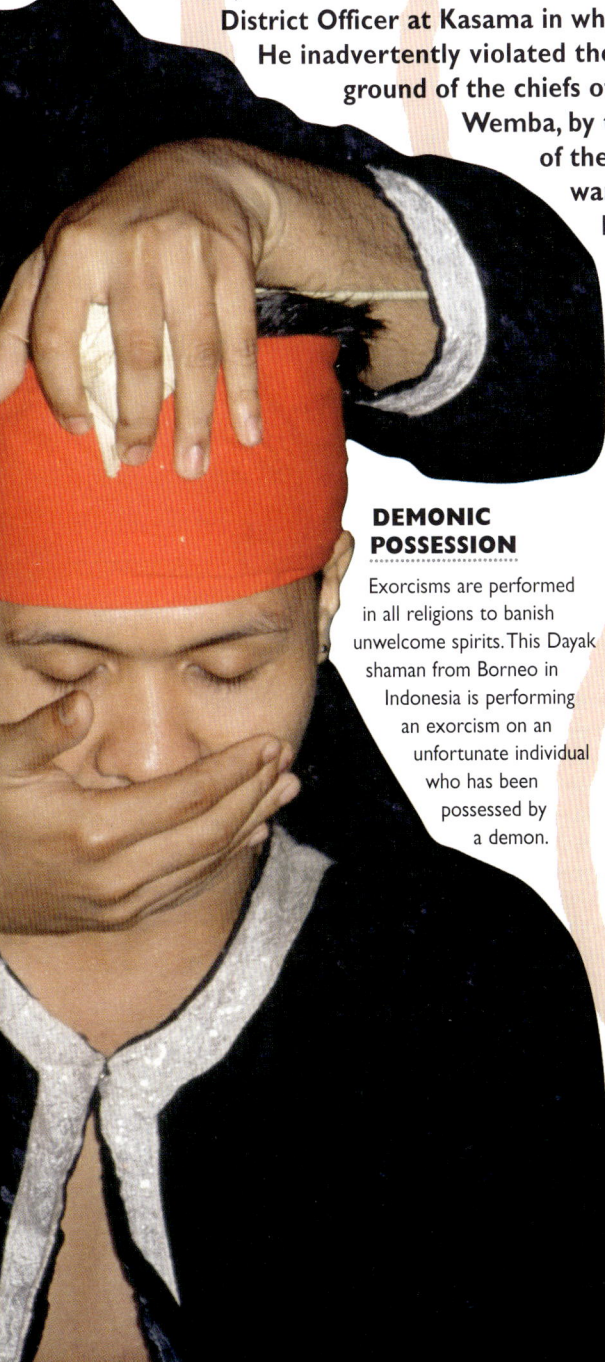

MODERN GHOSTS

In these enlightened times of scientific reason and logic, we might assume that most supernatural matters would by now have been sufficiently well investigated for us to take a rational view about them. One certainly might expect the belief in ghosts to be on the wane, but it is not. There has probably never been more interest, and ghostly manifestations continue to be reported. While many of these may be hoaxes, there is a growing weight of evidence to suggest that ghosts do exist.

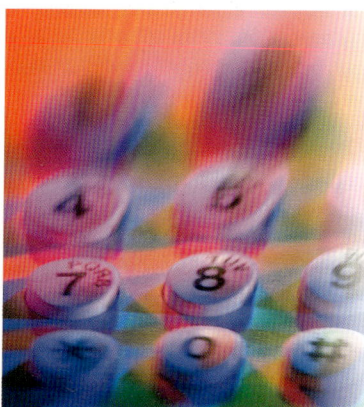

CAUGHT IN THE BEAM

In 1965, at Bluebell Hill, in Kent, three young girls were tragically killed in a motoring accident. The ghost of one of them still wanders the stretch of road, and the local police station often receives reports from drivers who think they have knocked someone down. When they get out to investigate they find no one there. Sometimes the girl hitches a lift and gets into a passing car but then mysteriously disappears. A similar story persists in Norway, where a sign has been erected on the roadside warning motorists not to pick up the ghostly hitchhiker.

MESSAGES FROM THE GRAVE

The answering machine of a Jules and Maggie Harsch-Fischbach from Luxembourg is allegedly haunted and regularly receives complex messages from dead scientists. Research into the life force that seems to occupy some inanimate objects suggests that they could be haunted by a previous owner who has left a mental imprint on them, psychokinetically.

FACES OF DEATH

In 1971, in the village of Bélmez in southern Spain, a ghostly human face suddenly imprinted itself on the pink floor tiles of a kitchen. When the family tried to rub off the troubled-looking face, its eyes opened wider and its expression saddened. The owner tore up the tiles and laid a concrete floor but another more clearly-defined face appeared. Experts in the paranormal were called in to investigate, and strange moaning sounds were recorded. Later, the house was found to be above an old cemetery.

THE WHITE HOUSE

The White House in Washington DC is haunted by a number of the past presidents of the United States. Several ghosts are attributed to Abraham Lincoln, who was assassinated in 1865. His distinctive image has been seen by such notable personages as Queen Wilhelmina of the Netherlands while staying there, and by President Reagan's daughter during his incumbency. Lincoln himself believed in spiritualism and attended several seances at the White House, which may account for his powerful presence still being felt there today.

FOOD FOR THOUGHT

An often overlooked aspect of ghosts is the powerful effect that wishful thinking can have on the human mind. The power of positive thought is very real and is taken seriously by doctors and scientists. After the death of a famous and much-loved person, such as Elvis, we long for them to live again. This sense of grief may be so strong that it could enable the human mind to externalize a familiar image which we then allow ourselves to believe is the ghost of the person we love.

DOES THE KING LIVE ON?

Elvis Presley (1935-77) became one of the most idolized entertainers of his time. To many people he remains the ultimate rock-and-roll star. When he died in tragic circumstances, many of his devoted fans refused to accept it. Since 1977, he has supposedly been sighted in a variety of places worldwide, not just in America.

GHOSTBUSTING

However sceptical we may be about ghosts, the vast number of reported sightings has encouraged some to take the subject seriously. Scientists have turned their attention to investigating paranormal phenomena, using a growing array of equipment and recording methods. Current research suggests that some form of energy (a by-product of electricity or magnetism) may produce ghostly manifestations. Until more conclusive evidence can be found, however, many will continue to believe in ghosts as supernatural beings from another dimension.

CHILL FACTOR

One of the most commonly experienced phenomena during poltergeist activity is a dramatic fluctuation in temperature, as was recorded during an investigation at Mulhouse in France. When ghosts appear, not only is the electro-magnetic field altered, but the ambient temperature can drop by 35°C. No wonder people who see ghosts often report a feeling of cold shivers. Such a drop in temperature can be recorded on portable infrared thermometers.

CAUSE AND EFFECT

Ghostly manifestations often occur together with recordable fluctuations in the Earth's electro-magnetic fields. Researchers use special equipment (above) to detect such changes, and some believe that these indicate the presence of ghosts. Others, including scientists at the Laurentian University of Sudbury in Ontario, Canada, believe that natural fluctuations in the Earth's electro-magnetic field can cause the human brain to hallucinate and thus 'create' its own ghosts. If this is true, then sites subject to magnetic fluctuations are likely to seem particularly haunted.

FOOD FOR THOUGHT

Despite the increasing sophistication of modern technology, including photographic and recording equipment, there is no conclusive proof of the existence of ghosts. If they exist, some form of evidence would surely have come to light by now. After all, a vast number of ghosts is purported to wander the Earth. It seems unlikely that ghosts are the spirits of dead people. Most reported ghosts are probably no more than self-induced images grown out of long-held superstitions.

CAUGHT ON FILM

Some researchers use infrared cameras to detect radiation from spirits, and also to photograph in the dark. More commonly, ghostly figures are unexpectedly caught in a photograph. The example shown here was taken in 1995, during the photographing of a fire at Wem Town Hall, Shropshire. When the picture was developed, this ghostly image appeared. It is thought that this could be linked with a previous fire at Wem in 1677, caused accidentally by a young girl. Critics suggest that such photos are merely accidental double-exposures, reflections, or even blatant frauds.